MW01139809

GOGO RORO FINDS HER GIFTS

Published by Davish Publishing, LLC
Knob Noster, MO 65305

Copyright © 2019 by Rousan J. Davidson
All rights reserved. No part of this book may be used or reproduced
in any manner whatsoever without written permission except
in the case of brief quotations embodied in critical articles or reviews.
Thank you for buying an authorized edition of this book and
for complying with copyright laws by not reproducing,
scanning or distributing any part of it without written permission.
You are supporting the writer and their hard work by complying
with such regulations.

Written by Rousan J. Davidson
Illustrated by Hayley Moore
ISBN: 978-1-7330980-0-7 (Paperback)
Printed in the United States of America
10 9 8 7 6 5 4 3 2 1
First Edition: June 2019

Dedicated to
my Grandmother
who is featured in this book as
"Abuela Rosa"
Rosa Gonzalez
(1947-2017)

GoGo RoRo

FINDS HER GIFTS

Written by Rousan J. Davidson
Illustrated by Hayley Moore

GoGo RoRo was one brilliant kid,

with many talents and many skills, she could do so many amazing things!

One morning, she awoke and raced down the stairs to find her Abuela Rosa and little brother Jean Bean talking about gifts.

With her birthday around the corner,
GoGo RoRo could no longer
hide her excitement.

"Abuela Rosa, Abuela Rosa!"
she yelled, "Tell me about my gifts!"

Abuela Rosa sat down with
GoGo RoRo and her little brother
Jean Bean and said,

"You will have to find them for
yourselves because they are
hidden. I can not tell you just
yet my children because
that would be forbidden."

GoGo RoRo and Jean Bean were determined to find all of the gifts.

They grabbed their gear and started
their hunt, hoping to find some
helpful hints.

They looked high.

They looked low,
and nothing had yet showed.

In every closet,

and
under
the stairs,

they still could not find them anywhere.

Up
in
the
cabinets,

inside
the fridge,

they even looked
in the toilet.

As bedtime drew near,

GoGo RoRo and Jean Bean
still had no clue where
the gifts might appear.

The next morning,
Abuela Rosa peaked into
the kitchen

GoGo RoRo and Jean Bean
walked to the table with
their heads down in shame.

They both looked around at all the mess they had made. "We just wanted to find all of the gifts," they sadly explained.

With a smile on her face, Abuela Rosa explained, "GoGo RoRo and Jean Bean, there were never any hidden gifts. I was talking about the gifts you both have from within;

like sharing,

and caring,

and encouragement."

You both have so many talents, many skills,

and can do so many amazing things,

but there is nothing as special as your God given gifts.

Your gifts were given to you
on the day you were born.

You do not have to
wait until your
birthday or
Christmas to receive
them anymore.

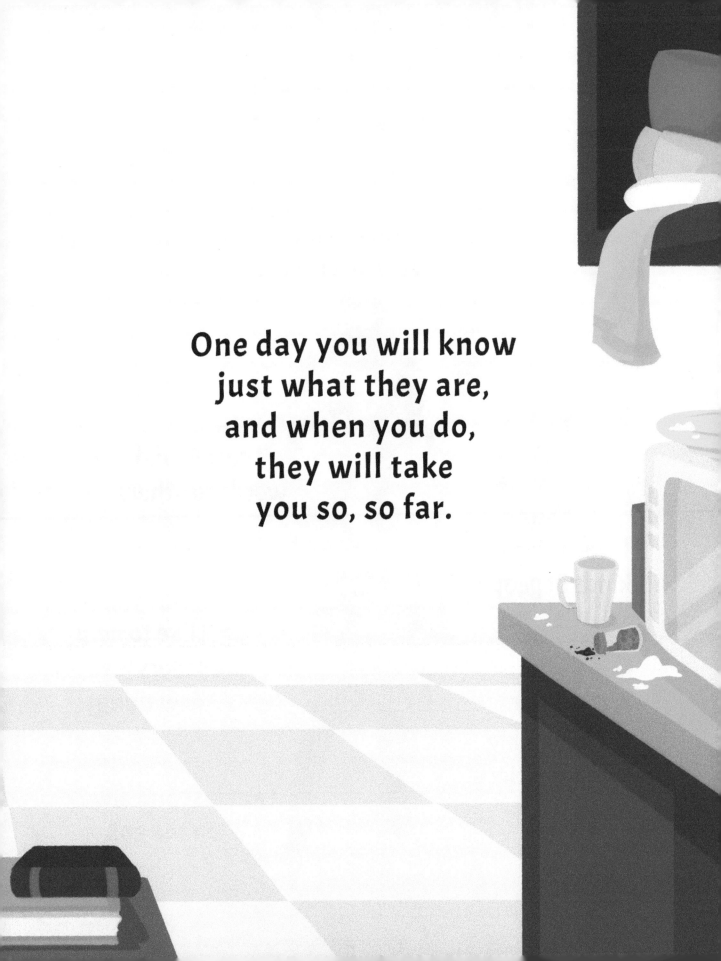

One day you will know
just what they are,
and when you do,
they will take
you so, so far.

"Abuela Rosa, Abuela Rosa! I found them!"

Wisdom
I always make good decisions.

Outlook
I look for the best in others.

Kindness
I speak kind words to others.

Love
I love all different kinds of people.

Leadership
I like to help others learn new things.

Creativity
I have a big imagination.

Movement
I am fast and always on the go!